Fall Is Here
Fall Harvest

by Sophie Geister-Jones

www.focusreaders.com

Copyright © 2021 by Focus Readers®, Lake Elmo, MN 55042. All rights reserved. No part of this book may be reproduced or utilized in any form or by any means without written permission from the publisher.

Focus Readers is distributed by North Star Editions:
sales@northstareditions.com | 888-417-0195

Produced for Focus Readers by Red Line Editorial.

Photographs ©: Shutterstock Images, cover, 1; iStockphoto, 4, 7, 9, 11 (top), 11 (bottom), 13, 15 (top), 15 (bottom), 16 (top left), 16 (top right), 16 (bottom left), 16 (bottom right)

Library of Congress Cataloging-in-Publication Data
Names: Geister-Jones, Sophie, author.
Title: Fall harvest / Sophie Geister-Jones.
Description: Lake Elmo, MN : Focus Readers, [2021] | Series: Fall is here | Includes index. | Audience: Grades K-1
Identifiers: LCCN 2019054506 (print) | LCCN 2019054507 (ebook) | ISBN 9781644933312 (hardcover) | ISBN 9781644934074 (paperback) | ISBN 9781644935590 (pdf) | ISBN 9781644934838 (ebook)
Subjects: LCSH: Harvesting--Juvenile literature. | Food crops--Harvesting--Juvenile literature.
Classification: LCC SB129 .G45 2021 (print) | LCC SB129 (ebook) | DDC 631.5/5--dc23
LC record available at https://lccn.loc.gov/2019054506
LC ebook record available at https://lccn.loc.gov/2019054507

Printed in the United States of America
Mankato, MN
082020

About the Author

Sophie Geister-Jones is a writer who lives in Minnesota. She enjoys spending time with her family, reading, and taking too many pictures of her dog.

Table of Contents

On the Farm 5

In the Store 8

On the Table 12

Glossary 16

Index 16

On the Farm

Fall is here.

Farmers are busy.

It is time for the harvest.

Harvest is when farmers gather **crops**.

Crops are plants we can eat.

In the Store

The farmers sell their crops.

People buy the food in stores.

People buy **pumpkins**.

People buy apples.

These foods are part of

the harvest.

On the Table

People eat the foods.

They bake pumpkin **seeds**.

People make **apple pie**.

People make apple juice.

The fall harvest is good.

apple pie

apple juice

Glossary

apple pie

pumpkins

crops

seeds

Index

A
apple pie, 14

C
crops, 6, 8

P
pumpkins, 10, 12

S
stores, 8